Love, Life, Death, Affection, Seduction, Destruction & Everything in Between

Poetry from the Pen of a Professional Amateur

Nathan Shepka

Copyright © 2011 by Nathan Shepka.

Library of Congress Control Number: 2011913454
ISBN: Hardcover   978-1-4653-0242-7
               Softcover   978-1-4653-0241-0
               Ebook   978-1-4653-0240-3

All rights reserved. No part of this book may be reproduced or transmitted in any form or by any means, electronic or mechanical, including photocopying, recording, or by any information storage and retrieval system, without permission in writing from the copyright owner.

This book was printed in the United States of America.

To order additional copies of this book, contact:
Xlibris Corporation
0-800-644-6988
www.XlibrisPublishing.co.uk
Orders@XlibrisPublishing.co.uk

Contents

Introduction v

Wounded World 1
Internet Romance 3
Love of an Angel 5
City Assassin 6
Astrological 8
Play the Joker 9
Rainstorm's Rage 11
She's Standing There 13
Forgive Me 15
Shadows 16
Laid To Rest 17
Jack of All Trades 18
Club Banger 19
Bearing Bars & Scars 20
Mexican Standoff 22
Victorious Anthem 24
Action Flick 27
Stones 29
Guard My Love 31
Castle Casts a Shadow 33
Like Money Leeches 36
Ten Tales 38
Four Forces 39
By Chance Romance 40
If Truth Be Told 41
Bitter But No Quitter 43
Old Jack 45
Tick Tock 46
Change of Heart 48
Short 49

Graveyard 51
Centre of Attention 53
Future Tense 54
By the Sword 55
Four in a Row 56
Wise 58
Appetise 59
You Are 61
After it All 62
On the Beat 64
Still 65
Grandfather's Chair 67
Bulletproof 68
Tranquillity and Silence 69
My Heart Is a Shell 70
Paid a Pittance 72
E-strangers 75
Colours 76
Land of Afar 77
Love or Lust? 78
Society's Stain 80
Brutal Blows 82
Inside Out 84
Dying Love 87
Staggered Speech 88
Miles Away 90
Mr Lover 92
Mother's Search 96
Winter's Wrath 98
Waiting for Heaven 99

Epilogue 101

To those with the genuine smiles
To Mum, Dad and E
To Gran, Grandpa and Nana
In loving memory of Papa
To Lil Cole, Stevie R, Davie and Grayham
To all my other friends and family
To the readers

Introduction

Dear reader,

This book was not written with a pen, it wasn't written with a typewriter, a word processor or even a quill and it certainly wasn't written with my blood, sweat and tears because believe it or not even books have health and safety issues. If only Uma had used a paperback in Kill Bill, the cuts would have been even more severe, and not just courtesy of the BBFC.

    Anyway, enough of the jokes. No, this book was in fact written with my own words, amidst a few cheeky little pop culture references thrown in for good measure and the occasional sweary word when civilised language doesn't quite carry the impact, (sorry Gran! But if only you knew what Grandpa said when you aren't around.)

    Not only is it an f-you in the face of all the people who have wronged me but a thank you to those who have enriched my life beyond the limited joy my own endeavours could provide.

    So read it from cover to cover and explore love, life, death, affection, seduction, destruction and everything in between. Don't try to look for hidden meaning, well not too hidden, it isn't cryptic, it's there in black and white if you look carefully.

    I can be a bleak bastard but also a cheerful chap filled with hope, the hope you do not deem a refund necessary by the end of this book.

To all the haters, I guess this is poetic justice? Right?

To all the lovers, I love you, and thanks,

                                                       Sheppy B-)

LOVE, LIFE, DEATH, AFFECTION, SEDUCTION, DESTRUCTION & EVERYTHING IN BETWEEN

Wounded World

The forests fall like wounded troops,
The ranks deplete, the bleeding wood,
Breaks like all the lovers' hearts,
Remove our world's breathing mask,
With savage axe, they're savaged more,
The pad for writers' pens to pour,
Their futile words scrawled on the page,
An outlet stream for all their rage

But what use is a writer's pen?
When in Iraq there's dying men,
Shot through the heart with mighty gun,
Their legs blown off before they run,
The evil set their ticking clock,
To kill the world and break the rocks,
That mould to build beloved land,
And grace the ground, on which we stand

Retaliation follows suit,
The politicians send in troops,
Whilst poisoned souls will preach their plight,
And hold the free world dead to rights,
With claims their freedom goes ignored,
Revenge attacks on every shore,
But nature's threat is mighty still,
Destroying towns at its free will

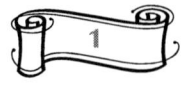

With reckless storms and vicious waves,
Fear that comes the end of days,
Payback for cutting nature's roots,
Denying time to bear the fruits,
That Mother Nature sought to give,
Inhabitants were free to live,
On forest gifts, enriching yield,
Giving earth the time to heal

Instead of melting all the ice,
And blowing up the east in spite,
As bombs rain down and troops deploy,
Deceivers suck out all the joy,
With brutal words and tainted rules,
Control the world with hands so cruel,
The earth is loaned to us on lease,
So turn the hatred into peace

LOVE, LIFE, DEATH, AFFECTION, SEDUCTION, DESTRUCTION & EVERYTHING IN BETWEEN

Internet Romance

A boring Sunday afternoon,
My day of rest,
But what to do?

A friendly "Hey" in online chat,
Ahh what the hell,
I'll say it back

A pretty girl, who lives close by,
We've never met,
I don't know why

A speedy hour slips away,
An endless stream,
Of things to say

A self confessed perfect ten,
With pale blue eyes,
Her name is Jen

A strong connection within weeks,
And then the query,
"Shall we meet?"

A word of strict motherly warning,
But I can feel,
A romance dawning

A shy exchange of smiling pics,
With firm intent,
To hit the flicks

An eager Sunday afternoon,
A crisp new shirt,
We're meeting soon

An unmistaken calling card,
A nervous sweat,
A trembling hand

A portly man waits by the door,
He strolls on up
And says "Hello"

A creepy smile reveals and then,
He introduced himself as Jen . . .

LOVE, LIFE, DEATH, AFFECTION, SEDUCTION,
DESTRUCTION & EVERYTHING IN BETWEEN

Love of an Angel

She lies in waiting, a bed dressed in silk,
Her skin is soft and pale like sweet milk,
Her eyes shine blue, like a tropic lagoon,
Her breasts are like flowers, rev'ling in bloom

Soft and tender, she beckons me over,
She whispers so softly, I pull her in closer,
My arms wrap around like entangling vines,
I'm lost in her trace, there's no track of time

Her scent is of strawberries, fresh from the fields,
Her arms like a jug and I am her yield,
With a face like an angel, from heaven above,
She's waits to receive my campaign of love

Her back arches proudly as the chasing begins,
The race to the finish, but I'll let her win,
Her gift becomes moist, like dew upon grass,
The night is our own, so our love's free to last

The neck of a swan, an elegant arc,
Legs like a dancer spread gently apart,
Her heart beats fast like a gay Congo drum,
She rests in my arms, when her river has run

ಬಿಲ್ಲ

City Assassin

A darkness cloaks the city,
Majestic skyscrapers glint,
The moon makes solemn crystal,
From climate beaten flint,
And twenty stone tales up,
Corners clogged with spider lint

Concrete colonies steadfast,
Proud patron saints they stand,
Pillars poised like prophets,
Unflinching royal guards,
The building peepers glazed,
With a tonne of tinted glass

A black assailant lurks,
Floats on silenced feet,
Noir nigger like a mourner,
Balaclava clad he creeps,
Pistol prized to puncture,
Slick, sleek, silver streets

He's armed to the teeth,
With contract killing tin,
Coal clothed panther leaps,
No more din than drawing pin,
And with sly gable DIY,
The Bureau parasite is in

LOVE, LIFE, DEATH, AFFECTION, SEDUCTION,
DESTRUCTION & EVERYTHING IN BETWEEN

Hinges shatter, frags scatter,
Corruption in a suit bespoke,
Charge ejects from Satan's spout,
Burnt munition stream of smoke,
As the Senate goes to scream,
Sterling slug jams in his throat

He makes attempt at sound,
Musters a gravely gargle,
Blood rushes up his gullet,
As his sole life passage mangles,
And as the liquid drowns,
He slowly starts to strangle

The blackened figure flees,
The fluid takes control,
Senate sinks helplessly,
To polished office floor,
Poisoned by his own,
Blood and gluttony both

Astrological

Water carrier bears his precious clay cruet,
An aquatic steam flows swiftly in through it,
The two fish tussle mid attuned array,
A flurry of scales adorn the floodway,
The ram barges brashly with thew-tearing horns,
In the spring of the year, in which he was born,
The bull catches rags, coloured red, in a rush,
In a stone coliseum that's brazen with dust,
The twins join together with unparting hands,
An eternal endurance that's free of disband,
The crab sharpens speedy, its shell strewing pincers,
The mark of the season that's halfway to winter,
The lion roars fiercely in a manner untamed,
Its face centred neatly in an unruly mane,
The maiden turns pink in the presence of love,
Her innocence white like a lone turtle dove,
The scales even out like a balanced enigma,
To weigh up the damage of life's luckless stigma,
The scorpion stings with a sinister tail,
For those who strike, its wrath will prevail,
The archer sits on his stallion throne,
A centaur who roams the land alone,
The sea goat swims through luscious creepers,
A bearded king, the landscape's keeper

LOVE, LIFE, DEATH, AFFECTION, SEDUCTION,
DESTRUCTION & EVERYTHING IN BETWEEN

Play the Joker

Palm cuts the pack,
Ace tops the stack,
The hands are soon dealt,
Good luck goes unfelt,
Once established intention,
There's no reinvention,
My turn comes around,
And like circus clown,
I play the joker

Teacher call the names,
Sense my claim to fame,
Awaited school play,
For the hero I pray,
But for that part I'm out,
Without shadow of doubt,
I play the joker

Fancy dress shop,
Jester hat prop,
Try it for kicks,
Seems like it fits,
Wear it forever,
Strained quips I deliver,
I play the joker

The object of ridicule,
Laughter is my fuel,
Their response a drug,
Find another mug,
No stand-up rehearsed,
The crowd has dispersed,
No longer the joker

The one who used to be funny,
Playing straight faced,
A new guy takes the hit,
Until his lines are spent,
Then he takes the fall
Popularity stalls

**LOVE, LIFE, DEATH, AFFECTION, SEDUCTION,
DESTRUCTION & EVERYTHING IN BETWEEN**

Rainstorm's Rage

The clouds above my head swell,
Befouled blister ready to burst,
A rumble roars within,
Like pent-up anger,
A jealous storm brews,
Swirling in the soup cauldron,
Flicker of light from the sunken abyss,
Then, like a fractured skull,
It cracks,
A sharply, spitely spear of light,
Cuts the air like killer's knife,
And then,
The first drop breaks the ground,
And ends the concrete's tarmaced drought,
A dozen more dots,
Disease the dusty, earthy crust,
The heavens unleash their yield,
Upon the evergreen fields,
A bucket of liquid broth, born in the sky,
The earthward blanket banquet,
Cures the flora's famine,
Sheets and sheets,
Drop like processed press,
Feeding from the celestial machine,
Flash!
A startling zap of strobeular light,
Darting sprites fill the night,
Canteens of cutlery stab the stage,

Forks and knifes in jabbing rage,
Trees tear, leaves obliterate,
A scurrage of leafy projectiles,
Hit the earth's hand like a long ward whack,
Raindrops tat-a-tat like a submachine,
Shoots become like submarines,
Like candy balls they crack the roofs,
Unrelenting and unresting,
Glass chandeliers pierce the pathways,
One huge blast like a Tyson thump,
Splits the sky like a sword,
Silver, sharp, slicing,
The heavens applaud,
As it cuts the cake,
Sprinkles splinter,
An electric overhead,
Beat, beat, beat,
Solar siphons smash earth's drum,
A rumbling symphony,
Orchestratic destruction,
God is the conductor,
Swipes his stick to command the bolts,
Charged with murderous volts,
Give earth an awakening jolt,
In the calm after the storm,
Everything smells new,
Quenched, drenched and refreshed

LOVE, LIFE, DEATH, AFFECTION, SEDUCTION, DESTRUCTION & EVERYTHING IN BETWEEN

She's Standing There

She's standing there,
Hourglass
Check the clock
Twenty past

She's standing there
Figurine
Action hero
Feminine

She's standing there
Slender legs
High heel boots
Clothing pegs

She's standing there
Curviture
Perfect breasts
Eyes that loure

She's standing there
God of love
Aphrodite
Turtle dove

She's standing there
Mesmerise
Teasing skirt
Hidden thighs

She's standing there
Cherry lips
Painted nails
Finger tips

She's standing there
Wait too long
Train has come
She has gone

LOVE, LIFE, DEATH, AFFECTION, SEDUCTION, DESTRUCTION & EVERYTHING IN BETWEEN

Forgive Me

Forgive me all those times I've told a little white lie,
Forgive me for the times when I said that I was busy,
Forgive me all those spiders I killed with callous hands,
Forgive me for favouring looks over internal beauty,
Forgive me for being vain and wearing out the mirror,
Forgive me for the harsh words expelled in heated arguments,
Forgive me for saying fat people should be thinner,
Forgive me for taking my parents grace for granted,
Forgive me for expecting friends to be near perfect,
Forgive me all those mistakes I made, despite me knowing better,
Forgive me the thoughtless jibes I threw at sensitive people,
Forgive me for looking close and picking out bad features,
Forgive me for being selfish and revolving the world around me,
For give my stupid ego when I should have remained grounded,
Forgive me for laughing at other peoples' problems,
Forgive me for creating them when I should have helped to solve them,
Forgive me for picking flowers that other hands have planted,
Forgive me for doubting the people closest to my heart,
Forgive me any betrayals and the excuse "I'm only human,"
Forgive me for being tactless when they ask "How do I look?"
Forgive me for breaking hearts without a second look,
Forgive me because I'll spread joy,
Any opportunity I get, I will help people,
I will forgive others; I will not let them down,
I will be the person everyone loves,
Forgive me for I cannot be perfect,
Forgive me for being me,
I am who I am,
I change for no one, unless for the better.

Shadows

Shadows are a lonely refuge,
A place to hide,
When all around you,
Scrambling for their independence,
Thank goodness for my blacked-out bedroom

Shadows are a winter blanket,
Hide the light,
Don't need to face it,
Taunting jibes and petty haters,
Thank goodness for my sainted basement

Shadows are a desert canyon,
Between two walls,
Escape the fandom,
Prying eyes and cruel spectators,
Thank goodness for my darkened walkway

Shadows are a dark escape,
When all your hopes,
Are in dismay,
The pressure builds, you waste away,
Thank goodness for the close of day

Laid To Rest

A glistening tear slid down her sweet face,
Like dew on a leaf, at the dawn of a day

Her eyes were like windows, deep into her mind,
That told a sad tale of a time left behind

The sky, like a shadow, hung over her head,
As she held in her hand, a rose coloured red

Her beloved lay down, in eternal rest,
A flag folded proudly, with medal on chest

She stepped one pace forward, and peered to the tomb,
Where a soldier so brave, once a babe in her womb

From a trench in the war, to a trench in the ground,
The guns fired loud, but she heard not a sound

The single red rose, slipped swift from her hand,
And landed so softly on now hallowed land

Retreating uneasy, with reluctance to part,
One more tragic hero, one more broken heart

Jack of All Trades

Thinks he is a jack of all trades, but he's mastered none,
Thought he was a plumber, but couldn't get his tap to run,
Thought he was a barber, but he balded an old lady,
Thought he'd play psychiatrist, but his patients called him crazy,
Thought he was an actor, but he soon forgot his lines,
Thinks he's Tim the Talking Clock, but he can't tell the time,
Thinks he's a Lothario, but women slap his face,
Thought he'd be an athlete, but he runs at half the pace,
Thought he'd be a poker champ, but he don't know how to play,
Thought he'd be a sat nav, but he doesn't know the way,
Thought he'd be an astronaut, but there's space between his ears,
Thinks he's a historian, but can't account for all the years,
Thought he'd be a gypsy, but fell out his caravan,
Thought he'd be a swimwear mod, but couldn't get a tan,
Thought he'd tell their fortunes, but couldn't see no tall, dark man,
Thought he'd play delivery boy, until he crashed the van,
Thought he'd be a judge, but he couldn't pass a sentence,
Thought he'd be a holy man but couldn't give repentance,
Thought he'd be a stand up, but he ain't no Benny Hill,
Thought he'd be a singer but he sounds like dying road kill,
Thought he'd be a muscle man, but couldn't lift a loaf of bread,
Thought he'd be a prophet but he couldn't predict the end

LOVE, LIFE, DEATH, AFFECTION, SEDUCTION,
DESTRUCTION & EVERYTHING IN BETWEEN

Club Banger

The bliss of the kiss from her crimson lips,
The swish and the swirl of her tantric hips,
She grinds and she bumps as he comes to grips,
With the buzz and the fuzz from his latest trip

The sparks and the barks as the clubbers shout,
The pace of the race as his heart clatters loud,
With cheers and jeers from the voice of the crowd,
As the tits and the bits of the dancers spring out

They prance and they dance in the midst of the trance,
No focus on static, no stare but a glance,
His eyes dart around like Le Shuttle dans France,
With the thrill of the pill comes a life or death chance

His head spins around like a beat doctor's disc,
A potion in motion, a zesty Bucks Fizz,
The cocktail concoction puts his brain in a tizz,
On insist from the dealer, the E was the biz

But the jump and the jolt of the merry-go-round,
Made a crunch and a punch as his heart muscle pounds,
He screamed out aloud, his distress call was drowned,
As he stumbled and tumbled and flopped to the ground

They stomp and they romp in their blind unaware,
They trample on ankles and evoke not a care,
Whilst he foams and he groans, his pulse hops like a hare,
'Til resign and relinquish his intake of air

The scream and the squeal of a siren alerts,
That the odds pose a loss when the drugs are bet,
And the pricks and the ticks of the post mortem tests,
Mean the drugs and the thugs are a customer less

NATHAN SHEPKA

Bearing Bars & Scars

Strict words emit from the mouth of rule,
Confusing wisecracks with wisdom,
Countless recitals of the riot act,
But the face of this cruel master,
Is one ravaged, like a relic, with time,
For the weary gristle and well worn features,
Carry a sadness made ever more obvious,
By the light that shines on teary eyes,
And a voice once with stern theatrics,
Stung with a shaky, quivering undertone,
A head from his bed, no desire to comb

Both harnessed with an undying duty,
To walk the canals of a complex castle,
And to tend to the foreign members,
Of a too often abandoned hallowed plot,
A jaded puppet master, who pulls the strings,
Of ball bearing, bar burdened cell dwellers,
An unsteady clink of his feet on the grills,
Keys bear a weight more great than they feel,
The keep of those society deemed,
An unhealthy unleash to roam the mean streets

LOVE, LIFE, DEATH, AFFECTION, SEDUCTION, DESTRUCTION & EVERYTHING IN BETWEEN

Home he goes in the darkest of hours,
One sorry meal in ungenerous glow,
Of a table lamp in a room filled with space,
The sad trip up the stairs to his final confine,
A bed with two sides but half unoccupied,
The cold breathes like spite as his arms,
Are the self comfort he is left with,
A sigh of defeat heats his hands for a second
His job is the wife he will always wake up to,
No lovingly made fresh eggs on a plate

And the days seem like decades, in a once treasured life,
Every minute a painful struggle for the end,
His uniform laid out in heroic attendance,
Chest graced with a crest of respectful address,
For sole purpose is clear, to be a watchful alert,
When the pat on the back isn't worth the regret,
The bank fills with pennies but it seems,
To him like copper coins are empty,
Like the soulless stone cages of leering offenders,
To which he spent his lifetime attending,
When final minutes with his cancerous kindred soul,
Slipped through his fingers like silicone,
Who fitted the bars to his own windows?
Someone's playing a cruel joke.

Mexican Standoff

Two bandit amigos,
Driven by evil

Uno lone ranger,
Mysterious stranger

Beard and grimace,
Embodied with hate

Pistol-a-brandish
Barrel outlandish

A whirlwind of ash,
A moment does pass

First to the draw,
Last to the floor

Bullets-a-plenty,
Gun never empty

LOVE, LIFE, DEATH, AFFECTION, SEDUCTION,
DESTRUCTION & EVERYTHING IN BETWEEN

But a few paces,
To blood-stained faces

Quick spin around,
One bastard down

Wound to the head,
Brain jammed with lead

Second man slaughtered,
Looks like he bought it

Third man triumphant,
From gun-slinger country

Walk to the sunset,
Reload for the next bet

Victorious Anthem

Take my hand; I will lead you there,
We'll walk over rainbows,
An arched pathway to peace

The sun beats down, but they won't beat us,
We feel warmth on our necks,
Freedom is our own again

The dark night that came before,
The people scorned,
Let them, they hate love

Wrapped in our own world, them in theirs,
Back in the womb again,
A bubble they won't burst this time
I'll be yours and you'll be mine

Ghosts that haunt us are in the past,
Said we wouldn't last
At least our hearts remain intact

Pearls of wisdom or jealousy green?
Our grass is green,
Theirs wilts like forgotten love

LOVE, LIFE, DEATH, AFFECTION, SEDUCTION, DESTRUCTION & EVERYTHING IN BETWEEN

Golden are the gates of heaven's palace,
Paradise silences their noise,
Drown out the shameful crowd

A stolen kiss, a night of bliss,
I'm taking you away,
They won't spit in our faces

Forbidden love? No one forbids me,
Forbidden fruit?
Yours is too sweet to deny

I'll bring you sunshine forever,
Purge their dark clouds,
No more stormy weather

Cast a shadow, we shall not hide in it,
Run like the wind,
Their shackles are not strong enough,
Said you weren't good enough

Your clothes never fitted
What does it matter?
Please don't become a piece of their putrid puzzle

Cradle me with your eyes,
I will be your antidote,
Their venom, we're immune to them now

Carry you over the rainbow, Promised Land
No pot of gold,
So what? Love's cup is full,
That's all I desire

We're there, top of the world,
No one knocks us down,
I can see their land, it is dark

Their fields lie bare,
Their love goes spare,
With ours, we share,
Unlikely pair,
We do not care

Our harps sing a note of love
Victorious anthem
Heaven above
Peace eternal
This is love

LOVE, LIFE, DEATH, AFFECTION, SEDUCTION,
DESTRUCTION & EVERYTHING IN BETWEEN

Action Flick

The way the villain rockets,
An exaggerated distance,
When arresting downtown perps,
They always pose resistance

When your faithful sidekick dies,
Amidst the opening shootout,
They always pair you up,
With some disrespectful loudmouth

The Captain's always grumpy,
And he threatens to suspend,
Takes your badge and gun away,
Until the movie's end

Always in a car chase,
Wreck your partner's silver jag,
Playing good cop, bad cop,
It's your in-joke running gag

Caught up in the crossfire,
Instigate a big explosion,
Drop your gun and run away,
In compulsory slow motion

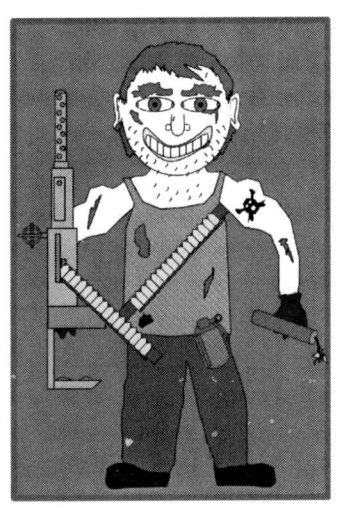

Fights up in a strip club,
Or in a dodgy, seedy bar,
A family member kidnapped,
This time they've gone too far

Movie ends with mayhem,
And an endless ammo weapon,
Rocket launchers, hand grenades,
The villain learns his lesson

A flame embodied showdown,
In an old abandoned plot,
Hand to hand, mano-a-man,
With a witty line to top

The confrontation is over
The head hoodlum has been killed,
You make up with the Captain,
And you always get the girl

Stones

Diamonds are a woman's first love,
I come second,
Collect them down the mine,
I'm paid pennies,
Such a priceless stone,
A pittance for my digging,
Hold in my hand but 1000 pounds,
Sit on some rich bitch's finger

Ruby is the name of my mother,
Proudest of parents,
Stern but a fair lady,
Wrinkles apparent,
But why not?
Not an easy life,
First a nun, then but a wife,
From God's servant to alcoholic's spouse

Emerald like a black cat's eyes,
Dart down the lane,
Spring to the chase,
Mouse maketh haste,
Agility is its virtue,
Tear up the air like a hurricane,
Rodent crushed by cruel teeth,
Happy feline grace-d with bloody fangs

Sapphire like the frost around my heart,
Never will melt,
Blue as the sea and the sky,
Defrost an iceberg,
My heart is but forever cold,
Open my chest freezer, fresh out of love,
Stocked with hate and remorse,
Tug the strings, no note sounds aloud

Stones may be priceless,
But they are lifeless,
Easy on the eye,
Wonder to behold,
But hard and so cold,
Sharp to the touch,
Cut like a knife,
Rounded by craftsmen,
Worn by the leaders of the land,
Stone on the hand,
Hard like their hearts,
Don't join the band,
March on your own,
Lead yourself alone

Guard My Love

Is there some reason why,
Whichever way I turn,
A dark cloud lies above,
Like a symphony unsung

But it never explodes,
In a shower of rain,
Dormant in my sky,
Like a victim of pain

A collation of illness,
A swollen flood vessel,
That refuses to shower,
When the month turns to April

An accomplice of acne,
That's ready to burst,
And cover my clothes,
With a spraying of puss

Because bad karma comes around,
When you spread your hate around the town,
Above your head a raincloud crown,
That bursts when you deserve to drown

But my raincloud stays there,
All through the year,
It leaks not a drop,
It cries not a tear

For I don't deserve it,
There's a burden inside,
And if sometimes I'm cruel,
It's the pain that I hide

But I'm not ready,
To let anyone in,
Not for real . . . not yet

My ribcage is the prison bars,
The prison bars around my heart,
To stop the treasure hunters' tempt,
To steal my heart without consent

And break it through with harsh contempt,
Without the notion to repent,
My name means gift, I'm heaven sent,
But life has left my will hell-bent

A love I do not wish to sell,
No one can take the tale it tells,
No soul can understand my head,
No known sites in length or breadth

You're free to take the guided tour,
Or browse my deep mental brochure,
But don't pretend to understand,
The complex myth behind the man

LOVE, LIFE, DEATH, AFFECTION, SEDUCTION,
DESTRUCTION & EVERYTHING IN BETWEEN

Castle Casts a Shadow

The ruins of a castle lay deep in the background,
The evening air smells fresh, yet claustrophobic

Its freedom stifled by familiar scent,
Foreground the concrete ornament

Puddles of water grace the ground,
That's been sober for so long,
An unusual sun cast days of drought

The green of the grass has been replenished,
With a shower from heaven's tap

He stands there alone, in the foreground
Looks like a perfect April picture,
For a calendar on the wall

A lone eagle cries a shriek of freedom,
Its wings part its body

An elegant glide to the tops of the trees
It settles for the night in a leafy abode

Rifle in hand, he wanders the lonely hillside,
The castle casts a dark shadow,
Of doubt on his safety

Like the grim reaper poised in position,
Behind the condemned
Not an eagle, but a crow

A black sign of betrayal,
And lust for one's own life force

Creeping across the land,
The castle's stare has no escape

To the forest ahead, roaming with his rifle,
The night blanket dampens the light,

Only a sense of direction,
And fearless facade to guide

What of the sprawling roots of eager undergrowth?
What of the dark's dismay?
What of the world beneath the evergreen cover?

What lies ahead? Only the eagle knows,
But not tonight,
Even he lies restful in his treetop paradise

Fresh from the gaze of the fractured ruins,
The gun barrel points northward

LOVE, LIFE, DEATH, AFFECTION, SEDUCTION,
DESTRUCTION & EVERYTHING IN BETWEEN

Like a compass its needle leading,
The way to the unknown

A shot reigns out,
The eagle has awoken

He falls to his knees,
Blue blood bleaches his royal attire

The forest floor shatters,
Like a heart, like a dream, like a soul,
Freedom be his own again

Like the wind in his hair,
Yet a comfortable garment,
Security, yet free of walls

The shot reigns every night hereafter,
A pale figure walks by the ruins

The eagle awakens upon the sound of the shot,
The royal chain has been sheared of its shackles,
Bound by no duty, but the duty to be free

Like Money Leeches

Government pay cuts, spending cuts, job cuts,
Proof of purchase shows they haven't bought much,
Billions borrowed, millions squandered,
Half our income big wigs launder,
UK's trousers have holey pockets,
No sooner said, they've went and lost it,
Cut the health or police or schools,
But leave the idle with millions cool,
Deadbeats claim for food and clothes,
Then rest their arse like disused hoes,
Bear the stink of weed and drink,
Morals washed right down the sink,
What an ironic term is employment benefit,
Should be "un" and employment to end it,
Cash on the hip, lies on the lips,
The Government should get a grip,
Stealing notes from hard working folks,
Shoving excuses down their throats,
But we can see through see-through lies,
They wash their hands and cut the ties,
That bind them to the average man,
Who has his pay snatched from his hands,
And given out to single mothers,
Who got a kid for fatter wallet,
And lazy fucks who stuff their face,
As decorated officers are disgraced,
And nurses, teachers and factory bods,
Are cast aside from paying jobs,
To fund the fun of brutal yobs,
Without a white tooth in their gobs,

As sinners sit and swig their beer,
And redundant workers stop and leer,
Our leaders lie in penthouse suites,
With everything to meet their "needs,"
A chauffeured limo to get to work,
But have the cheek to put fuel up,
These side-shed pricks with tailored suits,
And smarmy smirks, they seek to loot,
The workers of their hard earned cash,
To drive the economy to a crash,
I'd smash the smiles of their faces,
And put these bitches in their places,
As the Devil's hand they firmly shook,
Don't give the grafters second look,
Expenses paid at summonly click,
School fees, fam pics, yep, tick, tick, tick,
And at the close of spending review,
To sum it up, the words "fuck you,"
To keep the gullible public quiet,
While behind closed doors the rulers riot,
Decades, years, to pay their bills,
Siphoned cash at their free will,
Taxes raised and petrol raised,
And covered up with bullshit haze,
Leave the debt for the souls of tomorrow,
I hope their time is also borrowed,
As I wish death upon no man,
Except the scum that runs the land

Ten Tales

Chapter one, a babe in arms, a toothless grin,
Awake all night with deafening din,
Chapter two, a toddler crawls, a sea of toys,
Plethora of whys and countless falls,
Chapter three, first school day, packed lunch box,
Two grazed knees and woollen socks,
Chapter four, an acne siege, their first romance,
A frantic pen in May exams,
Chapter five, a shared abode, a kneeling pledge,
To answer with affirming "yes,"
Chapter six, a house enlarged, a pile of work,
A present from the mother stork,
Chapter seven, a five door car, a linen pram,
A trip to West coast caravan,
Chapter eight, a mid-life halt, they fly the nest,
Retirement with a gold wrist crest,
Chapter nine, a babe in arms, a wrinkled face,
Tireless grandchild fills their days,
Chapter ten, a final sleep, a toothless grin,
God will take a soul to keep,
A happy life is at an end,
Surrounded by beloved friends,
As teardrops well within their eyes,
With dying breath they say "Goodbye"

LOVE, LIFE, DEATH, AFFECTION, SEDUCTION,
DESTRUCTION & EVERYTHING IN BETWEEN

Four Forces

Fire burns with coalman's loot,
Burning bright, expleting soot,
Strike a match and light a candle,
Glowing beacon on the mantle,
Spark and flame and orangey glow,
Waxy residue, dripping slow,
My chest torch burns, with great desire,
Unless life's curse puts out my fire

Wind that blows me off my feet,
Chimneys whistle down the street,
Castle turrets endure the blast,
The wind whips out with vengeful lash,
Air to float a cheerful kite,
Aeolus rules with all his might,
What cometh to the men who sinned?
The answer's blowing in the wind

Earth that rests beneath my toes,
Haven where the flowers grow,
Support the trees and prep the land,
On which God's sacred house will stand,
Dig it up, the rough terrain,
Dry in sun and wet in rain,
Sand and soil provide my berth,
And all the creatures on God's earth

Water quenches fauna and flora,
Aquarius fills his prized amphora,
Cap Corelli drops his anchor,
Drain the juice of Nile's decanter,
I'm one drop in God's abyss,
Poseidon's force you can't resist,
When humans thirst just like they oughta,
The heavens open to send more water

By Chance Romance

A glance up from the scrawling page,
Working lunch at the coffee shop,
Our topaz eyes became engaged,
From either side of the restaurant

Those shy first words on brave approach,
A meeting set for evening's reign,
The firm remembrance of her face,
I'd never lift my head again,

As from that night that came before,
Refrain from tempt to scan the crowd,
For me she was my strength and core,
That year the wedding bells sang loud

A band of gold for her to keep,
A shiny penchant of my love,
But she's the keepsake that I need,
An angel sent from heaven above

The wedding night in Honey suite,
Champagne corks and smooth silk sheets,
Strawberries taste of Eden's sweets,
As tender lips excite to meet

And through the years of warm embrace,
Countless tantrums, tears and smiles,
The wrinkles write across her face,
A tale that true love's angel tells

LOVE, LIFE, DEATH, AFFECTION, SEDUCTION,
DESTRUCTION & EVERYTHING IN BETWEEN

If Truth Be Told

A woollen thread on denim thighs,
With which to weave deceiving lies,
A prong to fankle lengths of lace,
And cover up the candor's face

A sweater sewn to wrap around,
The shoulders of the foe to shroud,
But I'm not lying, if truth be told,
The tale I spun, was made of gold

Forget the boy, who once cried wolf,
This lie is like a sultan's jewel,
A complex maze of genius fibs,
To dig dictators in the ribs

They stuck me on a pedestal,
But I'm not one to be enthralled,
The lies bear burdens hard to hold,
For fear the sordid tale unfolds

One misplaced quip or fraudulent slip,
When tangled tongue feels loss of grip,
The victims seek to note a trend,
And alibis begin to bend

A plot that once was watertight,
Has fractured holes that let in light,
The blind begin to see the truth,
As untied ends will let cats loose

As the wool achieves unravel,
My failsafe takes a downward spiral,
The "foolproof" plans of mice and men,
Give way to meet a sticky end

And as I'm forced to soon come clean,
I see what farfetched lies there's been,
When on revenge you dig two graves,
A wicked path the untruths pave

For whether greed, or lust or guilt,
The lies will fall, from which they're built,
A coiled thread surrounds the proof,
But now the toothpaste's out the tube

My dirty laundry aired in public,
Skeletons breakout from the closet,
A word of warning to those who lie,
They'll pull the wool from o'er their eyes

Bitter But No Quitter

The days are black as night,
Forever cloudy in my sky,
My mother mourns my every move,
My father keeps a watchful eye,

But I'm way out of his vision range,
Too far afield to see,
They watch the dust cloud settle,
As I commence my war with speed,

Time is my only restraint,
To get my do list done,
I saddle up apocalypse horse,
And watch those haters run

I'll make a buck or a billion,
But I'll make far more than you,
I'll spend my living minutes,
Keeping out the dole cheque queue

I don't need to scrounge,
Or steal the payers' keep,
Or stuff my face with freebie treats,
Succumb to guzzler's greed

No man shall pay my boardings,
No man shall pay my food,
I sign the deal, collect the cheque,
It's all for greater good

The knowledge that I'm making,
More than in these bitches' banks,
Keeps the smile on my face,
As I inspect my ranks

A troop of loyal workers,
More a fan club than a force,
I marry my childhood sweetheart,
Cause true love don't file divorce

To all you cider swiggers,
And two faced, two timing sluts,
Keep your coke and junk food fund,
Cause I don't give a fuck

And as you sit there spacing,
In a council rented chair,
Remember that I rule the world,
And you haters way down there

You ripped to shreds my confidence,
With your ever jeering smirks,
You tormented me for bookworm looks,
And dragged me through the dirt

But all your jibes and petty threats,
Don't matter, not a jot,
Cause when I fuck the world this time,
I'll be the one on top

LOVE, LIFE, DEATH, AFFECTION, SEDUCTION,
DESTRUCTION & EVERYTHING IN BETWEEN

Old Jack

Old Jack knows his time has come,
Baked in sun with hipflask rum,
His feet plod like a beating drum,
Assures his spouse with skyward thumb,
A parting hug and one last kiss,
Walk two by two into the mist,
A soldier's hat and starting stripe,
His rifle slung with which to snipe,
Into the fields where poppy's bloom,
Red like blood and black like doom,
A squatting stance with rifle north,
When whistle hoots he marches forth,
The dust explodes like desert sand,
And on the three stripe's strict command,
He weaves the field like jungle's snake,
Surrounding earth erupts and quakes,
As shots pour from his weapon's spout,
The slugs implode and pain rings out,
Buckshots seer with deafening snap,
The foes surround, their bodies capped,
With point-blank punch from Hitler's guns,
No route to go, to cut and run,
A shot reigns close and jams his head,
With iron ration's dose of lead,
Gray matter divided o'er the plain,
The German's call it scatterbrain,
A letter read to widow's weep,
Inform her that her love's asleep

Tick Tock

Every waking minute enclosed in office claustrophobia,
A solitary box with a view of what might have been,
The pointless pedestal of office chair,
Fashioned from an elephant's back,
By bill payer or bum bearer,
They were always going to get their pound of flesh

Like an office recluse with ballpoint pen and paper stack,
Not printed notes but figs and facts,
Emerge like a gremlin but for a weary trip,
To the tea machine for ineffective caffeine kick,
Tea break is over before a breath,
Back to the dread and the desk

Deadlines hang like reaper's wrath,
The cloaked figure in clerical black,
Scrounging for the market stats,
A late night lesson in how to stay awake,
The mile high pile is tall but hours are small,
And the clock hands insist on going at double time,
Despite the pay deciding not

With the minute reluctant to linger,
And the candle scorched at opposite ends,
The hours slip helplessly through fingers worked to the bone,
A weary wife ushers the kids to bed,
But this wasn't in your mental sketch?
Forever dabbling in the mundane?

LOVE, LIFE, DEATH, AFFECTION, SEDUCTION, DESTRUCTION & EVERYTHING IN BETWEEN

Your yawn all but swallows the room,
As borrowed pennies fail to fill the bank,
When swiped away before the penny drops,
The piggy bank slot lies in wait,
But someone left a hole in the bottom,
Forget the impossible superior set goals,
The ink ran out, now so should you

Stare up at the sun, others head to work,
Just another day at the office? Not for you,
Reunite with freedom, the desk drawer locked for good,
And the suit banished to the confines of a restricting wardrobe,
Imprisoned behind the R&R wear,
Monday morning comes around but you do not care,
Desk job jockey no more,
Live every day like it's your last,
Forgive the sinners of the past,
Don't let time waste away,
In an endless squint at a square eye inducing spreadsheet

Change of Heart

NATHAN SHEPKA

Drunkard lying in the gutter,
Eyelids closing like a shutter,
Couldn't fall down any further,
Death is near, cause life is murder

Man just couldn't hold his liquor,
Wife has left him, now he's bitter,
Given up, just like a quitter,
Step over him, just like he's litter

Who will save this fallen man?
Cry for help, but they just ran,
He'll find his good Samaritan,
God will lend a helping hand

Eyelids open, heart at peace,
Picked himself up off the street,
Just couldn't pay the heaven's lease
So now he's back upon his feet

God said his life ain't over yet,
One more drink, he would regret
Difference between his life or death,
Is one wrong move, one misplaced step

Knocked upon his ex-wife's door,
Said he missed her, that he swore
Promised to love her evermore,
He's back now in her heart once more

Next time your life is in the dark,
See and have a change of heart,
The sun is out, your sky is black,
But life hits hard, so hit it back

LOVE, LIFE, DEATH, AFFECTION, SEDUCTION,
DESTRUCTION & EVERYTHING IN BETWEEN

Short

Pence short of a pound,
Drink short of a round,
Noise short of a sound,
Fall short of the ground

Class short of a clown,
Drip short of a drown,
House short of a town,
Up short of a down

Cloud short of a sky,
Wing short of a fly,
Peep short of a pry,
Tear short of a cry

Poem short of a line,
Clock short of the time,
Word short of a rhyme,
Steak short of its prime

Grave short of a stone,
King short of a throne,
Leg short of a bone,
Boat short of a rowin'

Hood short of a bow,
Truck short of a tow,
Stones short of a throw,
Green short of a go

Leaf short of a tree,
Sting short of a bee,
Wave short of the sea,
Break short of being free

Love short of a heart,
Swing short of a park,
Dog short of a bark,
Angel short of a hark

Card short of a pack,
Break short of a back,
War short of Iraq,
Tic short of a tac

Blind short of a bat,
Brim short of a hat,
Flea short of a rat,
Spoil sort of a brat

Spare short of a part,
Wheel short of a cart,
Tip short of a dart,
Wal short of a mart

Pea short of a pod,
Greek short of a god,
Buff short of a bod,
Fish short of a rod

Dip short of a bend,
Foe short of a friend,
Mail short of a send,
You've come to the end.

Graveyard

The graveyard, a silent field of corpses,
A crop that no one wants to harvest,
Blocks of stone in uniform lines,
Fallen soldiers but not forgotten,
Heartfelt visit once a week,
A sob or two, a bunch of roses,
Their flowers have long wilted,
But their roots remain,
A scrawling note and RIP
Legacy left behind, a moment in time,
A million tears flood the ground,
But not when darkness falls,
The lifeless limbs rest alone,
The only life is by wrong turn,
In which the victims turn and run,
No one dare walk the land,
Where buried bodies waste away,
The flesh rots but hard and fast,
Their soul lives in their loved one's hearts,
A faded black and white,
Face of the angel centre stage,
Dated, boxed and locked away,
The snapshot and the casket both,

One for keeps and one for God,
Regret the day when those who remain,
Resign their case and join the ranks,
Fresh new stones of speckled marble,
All assigned to earthy plots,
No one left to remember,
Their glory days forgotten,
Their smiles and eyes reduced to dust,
But what of life if it ends with death?
Enrich the soil and start again,
Leave your legacy behind,
A mark upon the entire world,
Stamp your emblem on their hearts,
Whether verse or tale or rhyme,
Your brand be left in time,
For those you loved will long be gone,
But your name can live to help the souls,
That struggle through their own adventures,
Leave your life's lessons,
And teach the world,
Commanding from the ground,
Be the head of every stone

LOVE, LIFE, DEATH, AFFECTION, SEDUCTION,
DESTRUCTION & EVERYTHING IN BETWEEN

Centre of Attention

Slimline figure with a slimline tonic,
Struts like she owns the world,
Her thighs magnetic to men's eyes,
They drag across the room in lustfull gaze,
Lost in her, their eyes will glaze,
Women turn away, repellent in disgust,
Jealous of the catwalk queen, the men are keen,
They crowd around, she settles down,
She's centre of attention

She tosses her hair in carefree manner and pouts,
But she's got a head upon her shoulders,
She is the peacock, so she'll put on the show,
They all desire and expect, but she's unfazed,
Uninterested by their sexual jeers,
Unflattered by their winks and cheers,
Unflinching at their groping hands,
They can touch, they cannot have

Her pampered hand stays shy of her purse,
They irrigate her vodka lust,
But that is her only desire,
A sickly liquid, straight up shot,
Filtered though the icy blocks,
A chilled stream flows down her throat,
She looks up, awaits another,
Ten drinks down, she smiles seductively,
She is sober but they are love drunk

She brushes off their stealthy hands,
Sliding t'wards her outstanding assets,
Their hearts sink like a punctured boat,
She's gored a hole, and let them flood,
She approaches but a solitary table,
One solitary man, she begs the question,
"Do you want me?" "No," he assures,
She is his for the night,
And maybe tomorrow's night,
She'll see

Future Tense

Peer inside, crystal ball,
Future tense, see it all,
Tall dark man, long black coat,
Shallow water, stranded boat,

Mary had a little lamb,
Drowned at sea, could have swam,
Forgive my sins, say your prayers,
Underwater, algae layer,

Pale as white, like a ghost,
Hidden depths, wouldn't float,
Ankle trap, cunning weeds,
Wrap-around, no warning heed,

Leaning over, overboard,
Anchor drop, water's hoard,
Good advice, fast forget,
Attention lost, deep regret,

Crystal ball, future tense,
Daughter's death, can prevent,
See it clear, see it well,
Cautious words, the crystal tells

LOVE, LIFE, DEATH, AFFECTION, SEDUCTION,
DESTRUCTION & EVERYTHING IN BETWEEN

By the Sword

Be it by the sharpened sword,
The men who cut, themselves they forge,
A darkened path, that's free of light,
When set upon their vicious plight,
To purge the land's opposing souls,
Drowned in blood and raid their gold

Be it by revolver's jolt,
Like shiny steel, their heart's a Colt,
The bullets grim, a drop of death,
To weed the armies from the earth,
That seek about to scorch their dream,
And overthrown their King and Queen

Be it by their trusty steed,
To crush the lungs by which they breathe,
And crack the skulls with callous hooves,
To see it forth they shall not lose,
With their shoes and whips and shackles,
Ride the death cart into battle

Be it by the poison dart,
That drains the life force from their heart,
And rips the smile upon their face,
A tip of death to end the chase,
The struggle in their final moment,
To squeeze the air in though their throat

Be it by the icy stare,
That kills its foe without a care,
Before it tears their world apart,
With thoughtless worlds straight to the heart,
They pick the lock and turn the key,
To set all their emotions free,
The pain of words is just as strong,
As any blade or bow or prong,
That staves the lies in love of truth,
And calls the countries to a truce

Four in a Row

Chemists distribute the pills,
Money man, collect the bills,
Rollercoaster, seek the thrills,
Jack and Jill fell down the hill

Wrestler pull a power slam,
Hit the beach, collect a clam,
High my five and strike the palm,
Do the splits like you're Van Damme

Ballet dancer bust a move,
Practise maketh one improve,
Egocentric, what's to prove?
Ghetto jam, get in the groove

Big Ben clock doth tell the time,
Rapper spitting out a rhyme,
Exchange a nickel for a dime,
Granny Smith is past her prime

**LOVE, LIFE, DEATH, AFFECTION, SEDUCTION,
DESTRUCTION & EVERYTHING IN BETWEEN**

Patience bailed, it's the last straw,
Giddy up, Quick Draw McGraw,
Beat him up, his face red raw,
Witness detailed what he saw

Field of death, here lies the poppy,
Drunken painter, work looks sloppy,
Back up data, burn a copy,
Rich man's daughter acting stroppy

Eden bears a bitter fruit,
Cheating girlfriend got the boot,
Robber ran with all the loot,
Students study, get astute

Old and new and blue and borrow,
Banish grief and bar the sorrow,
Save your judgement for Gomorrah,
Live life like there's no tomorrow

Wise

Wrinkles run ragged across his old face,
Grooves like a river bed,
Wore away the youth,
Eyes sunken 'tween sand dunes,
Suns curse been no use,
Farther he fled, skin beaten red

Into the West where steeds grunt,
Shade is the safe house,
Solitude from sky's pry,
Scorch even a field mouse,
Hide amongst the prairie grass, relief is at last

Trouble has brewed, but he refuses a taste,
An unwelcome old friend,
A frequent acquaintance,
Scorned women, foul temper,
Grace the pictures of the past

Guilty of living, no need to stand trial,
Red hot reputation,
Glazed with fragile facia,
Could fool even a joker,
Seasoned with the seasons,
Clearing the dust, retribution a must

Dark deals with the devil are anti-fruitful,
Pay in tears likely,
Strike with a hot iron,
Play away from home,
Unfaithfulness unforgiven,
Sombre gaze,
Replace seductive eyes,
Life of lessons,
Less the achievement,
Of a warm hand on his cheek,
Should that sun disappear

LOVE, LIFE, DEATH, AFFECTION, SEDUCTION,
DESTRUCTION & EVERYTHING IN BETWEEN

Appetise

Come in, come in, the doctor begs,
Take the weight up off your legs,
Sit upon the comfy couch,
Sit up straight, try not to slouch,
Relax your mind and breathe in deep,
Your secret's safe for me to keep,
Let time flow by without a care,
Into the watch you weakly stare,
A sleeping pill upon a string,
Your eyes draw tight, it pulls you in,
I think it's time to enter slumber,
Those eyelids pose a heavy lumber,
Surrender to my golden charm,
I promise you shall see no harm,
Arriving in the land of Nod,
Your frozen mind, I will defrost,
Think of chocolates, sweets and cakes,
The wondrous smell, all freshly baked,
Now read the danger sign ahead,

If those you eat, you'll end up dead,
Rearrange your shopping cart,
Banish sickly strawberry tarts,
See yourself becoming thinner,
When you're eating less for dinner,
Forget the pain of sugar-free torture,
You're walking through an apple orchard,
Despite your sweet tooth's sickly crave,
The cakes are in Aladdin's cave,
Fruit salad graces every plate,
Their sweetened juice is to your taste,
Knock down the house of Hans' and Gretel,
Ignore the treats the sweet shop pedals,
When you awake you will have changed,
Your mind inside a different frame,
My fingers click like dawn's alarm,
The thought of cakes has been disarmed,
The doctor tells his patient "go"
He's finished with his mind-control

LOVE, LIFE, DEATH, AFFECTION, SEDUCTION,
DESTRUCTION & EVERYTHING IN BETWEEN

You Are . . .

You are the one I kiss goodnight,
You are my wings when I'm in flight

You are the breath upon my cheek,
You are the treasure that I seek,

You are the river that runs deep,
You are the one I choose to keep

You are the temple, in which I pray,
You are the best part of the day

You are my tap when I need water,
You are the breeze when it gets hotter

You are the one I ask to dance,
You are the face of true romance

You are the petal on the flower,
You are the pleasure I devour

You are my light when filled with grief
You are my staple pain relief,

You are the pillow in my bed,
You are a place to rest my head

You are the lining in every cloud,
You are the one of whom I'm proud

You are the blazing summer sun,
My solace when the day is done

After it All

Lay still like dusk's horizon,
Settle for a moment,
Like the scarlet sky,
Before the blanket drops,
Rest like a concrete rock,
Too hard to lift my head,
Sunken shoulder, old tin bed,
Cabinets of corpses,
Wall to wall in dead

My bloodshot eyes,
Are tucked away,
Behind skin coloured curtains,
A panel to the outside world,
Skylight like a perfect picture,
A wind collects around my heart,
Mini chest tornado

Last drops of life,
Are poured into a floating beacon,
Mist like marshland camouflage,
Floats like a helium sphere,
Smells like a newborn baby,
Leaving this damaged earth,
My little space cadet

Drift through double glazing,
I turn white and blue,
Like my new found friends,
Soul soldiers on,
Free as a bird,
Clouds tell 1000 words,
Pictures painted in cotton fluff,

LOVE, LIFE, DEATH, AFFECTION, SEDUCTION, DESTRUCTION & EVERYTHING IN BETWEEN

I'm in God's gallery now,
Celestial pipes in perfect pitch,
Light like never before,
The starving never hunger,
Thirsty throats quenched,
Eyes are blue again,
Golden instrument granted

Chord to make the coldest cry,
One note to seal,
A broken heart,
Angelic voice melts the harshest man
The beasts become tame,
Sky situated castle,
With no battle ground,
No defending ranks,
The bows and pricks,
Replaced by harps,
My day trip is tomorrow,
A presence at my wake,
Their shoulders draped with black,
I am the only one in white

NATHAN SHEPKA

On the Beat

Cop on the beat
Size twenty feet
King of the street

Little white packet
Fifty in wallet
Slip to the pocket

Merc roll on by
Worldly despise
Turn a blind eye

Keep kids in college
Pay off the mortgage
Powdery haulage

Ship in the port
Deal with the court
Sentence abort

Shiny new medal
LSD pedal
In-patient referral

Overdose son
Streets overrun
Damage is done

Eyes start to weep
Heart start to bleed
Resign from the beat

Still

We lie still,
Calmer than settled waters,
The clouds are scattered across the sky,
Strewn carelessly like frantic clothes,
We lie still,
The lips on her sun kissed face,
Like velvet petals on a rose

We lie still,
Like the garden hammock,
When the wind is too weary to blow,
A gentle breath is but all it can muster,
We lie still,
The sun wraps around us with tender arms,
The golden ray's comforting cuddle

We lie still,
Buds crack like eggshells,
Blooms stretch t'ward sun's gaze,
Open and relaxed, well rehearsed speech,
We lie still,
Breathe the air with added appreciation,
Like a sweet scent just beyond reach

We lie still,
And all I can hear,
Is the pat of her heart,
In the shell of my ear,
As my head rests against,
Her magnificent chest,
Like a proud crested bird,
It's the place I love best,
When the cold winter chill,
Takes its frosty, harsh grip,
I hibernate with her,
And cling to her hips,
In the storm or the calm,
At each end of the year,
My rock is her arm,
Whether smile or tear,

We lie still,
The whole world sleeps,
With us it sleeps,
We lie still,
Even if the world is at war,
Even if the skies rumble,
Even if the concrete quakes,
It can crumble around us,
But we'll be still, all the same

LOVE, LIFE, DEATH, AFFECTION, SEDUCTION,
DESTRUCTION & EVERYTHING IN BETWEEN

Grandfather's Chair

I sit like a King in my Grandfather's chair,
A home once so warm, now filled with despair

The fire filled with ash, the garden unkempt,
The silver unpolished and the tiles unswept

The Grandfather clock doesn't chime anymore,
Ticked not but a tock since he last closed the door

A jaunt to the shops for butter and milk,
His heart like a flower, when neglected, it wilts

His beloved lay peaceful, deep under the ground,
The day since she passed, his smile's upside down

He took up his cane and limped o'er the street,
With sorry sad eyes for the people he'd meet

All the flowers and cards contained in the world,
Couldn't bring her back, his bonnie old girl

His heart split in two like a branch from a tree,
Finally in heaven with his love he would be

And as I sit here looking up to the wall,
If their picture could speak, a tale it would tell

ಶಿಧಿ

NATHAN SHEPKA

Bulletproof

Saggy physique like exertion forgotten,
What it is to graft and sweat,
But in my mind I'm a superhero,
Forged of steel with Kevlar chest

A scampering wimp should duel arise,
A flitting ferret with fearful fever,
But in my head a daring victor,
That turns a cynic to believer

A cursed trait of rosy flush,
When perfect ten smiles straight ahead,
My words consumed by bashful blush,
As beauty rears its pretty head

But in my eyes I'm Casanova,
"Kiss my quick thy Romeo!"
My LL Cool J skills unrivalled,
A Kama Sutra connoisseur

A sarcy grin gives way to sorrow,
Spectators undermine my fears,
In the flesh they're tragic halt signs,
But in my mind they're crocodile tears

And whilst I hope the taunts subside,
When the doubters say that I'm no use,
The truth that lies beneath the Kevlar,
Is that underneath I'm bulletproof

LOVE, LIFE, DEATH, AFFECTION, SEDUCTION, DESTRUCTION & EVERYTHING IN BETWEEN

Tranquillity and Silence

Tranquillity and silence
Broken by violence
Scared to surrender
Fear of defiance

Hand raised higher
Older not wiser
Savagely beaten
No villain demiser

Mirror is broken
Child is awoken
Jaded reflection
Wounds are re-opened

Time is a healer
Bruiser concealer
Reluctant retreat
Heart without feeling

Freedom is golden
Suitcase-a-holding
No more forgiving
Victim disclosure

Bully abolished
Fear is demolished
Life is restored
Improvement acknowledged

My Heart Is a Shell

NATHAN SHEPKA

I can hear them outside,
The merriment moves me,
They drink and they laugh,
And they're making sweet music

But I am alone,
My castle is empty,
My heart is a shell,
But with burdens aplenty

My workload is stacked,
Right up to my neck,
I need someone's loving,
If it is but a peck

A knock at the door,
Should I join their party?
The dancing is merry,
The food looks so hearty

A gracious decline
I don't feel their cheer,
It's always the same,
At this time of the year

The sun shines above me,
In my head it's black
It's bright on the outside,
But dark in my heart

For I've lost my soul mate,
The love of my life,
She was my angel,
Above being my wife

LOVE, LIFE, DEATH, AFFECTION, SEDUCTION, DESTRUCTION & EVERYTHING IN BETWEEN

Left me for another,
Did that I deserve?
I had me one purpose,
For her but to serve

She took it for granted,
I still miss her so,
I could join the party,
But my heart would not go

For it is here waiting,
The day she returns,
When she knows I'm best,
And the one she should love,

I miss her soft kisses,
The smile on her face,
Her bed still lies empty,
I'm keeping her place

She broke me in two,
But that I forgive,
Her beauty unrivalled,
In my memory she lives

As I lie in the dark,
Hidden in my four walls,
One knock at the door,
Could brighten it all

But it won't be her,
She's left me forever,
If I don't make it through,
May the Lord God forgive her

Paid a Pittance

They bravely sign their names on deadly dotted line,
Sign their life away to another place and time,

Pockets filled with worthless weight of tarnished brass,
Hands with poison pellets, nostrils smell the scent of gas,

Ten mile trek in sweating angry sun as blisters bleed,
Orders from the silver suits to rid of all opposing creeds,

The weight of worry lies heavy yet upon their back,
And killing tools with gutless blades in duffle sack,

Back at home in oak stained offs and leather briefs,
Sit cigar bastards eating tar and playing chiefs,

The money rolls like ocean sways, a tidal wave,
As bankrupt wife of fearless man sees funds go stray,

The soldiers live another day in dusty desert stench,
Compared with bureau rats they're paid in merely pence,

And as they make the hopeless trek through featureless battlefield,
The swanky strips pretend to break a sweat on comfy playing field,

A minute of their time is another thousand in the bank,
Whilst the bleeding troops take another bullet in the back,

And their wives wait each day for the monthly letter home,
Whilst footballers' wives sip the champs and cheer the champs of another goal,

LOVE, LIFE, DEATH, AFFECTION, SEDUCTION, DESTRUCTION & EVERYTHING IN BETWEEN

They dip themselves in tan and blonde like noble wags,
Then wait for team cap to make them rich like money slags,

They sit well back on leather couch and spread their legs,
As redundant worker takes up a cardboard box and begins to beg,

There's a world of difference between England squad and army squad,
But supporters cheer the team that chase the goalward ball,

They go home at night to the pleasures of a bubble bath,
Whilst the troops lie in wait to feel a bombshell blast,

And blonde bombshells snuggle up to rich physique,
And sorry souls pick fallen friends up off the street,

But I say take the million pounds back for treading grass,
And give it to the British bods, who patrol Iraq,

Cut the cash artery of all the useless championed defenders,
Make them pay in blood like our country's defenders,

As whilst the slutty, unfaithful, moral lacking men,
Are off philandering their way through the district lit with red,

And their wives turn a blind eye to keep their million dollar jag,
The soldiers' wives wait for saddening news of the latest attack,

Forget these soldiers of fortune and remember the real fighters,
Support the soldiers, not the teams, hold up your lighters,
And thank the troops for trying to make our world brighter,

They roll in dirt, not dollars,
Change in shacks, not fancy, gold-tap locker rooms,
But they are stuck in shacks,
Whilst the rich rake in stacks,
Tomorrow it's pay-day,
For some it's d-day,
Something's wrong with the world,
I'd call a doctor but you paid them off,
Ask a sportsman to save lives,
You pay them enough

E-strangers

They yearn for love as it was before,
With its tender moments alive once more,
A love so bright it dimmed the stars,
But the train derailed and scored the scars,
Upon the lovers broken hearts,
The decision made to split and part

The ampersand once ajoined their names,
Their wedding pics once graced the frames,
Upon the happy household walls,
Until the moment darkness falls,
When all their days turn into night,
And love's replaced with snarl and spite

Don't try to run before you walk,
Atonement comes before a fall,
The love laid waste to prenup claim,
The scapegoat always gets the blame,
Two hearts were once entwined as one,
Now loves course has hast'ly run

Love is like harmonious song,
But truth 'comes lie and right goes wrong,
The lovers soon come strangers be,
And part in half like the red sea,
Bitter brawls and shouts and bawls,
A court fought battle ends it all,
To what once set as sweet adore,
Came strangers housed on separate shoes

Colours

Red is the rose, entwined on the fence,
Copper is worth not a pound, but a pence
Gold is the ring, I place on her finger,
White is the light where the moths like to linger

Blue is the shade of the sky and the sea,
Green is the grass and the fields and the trees,
Amber the light that comes in the middle,
Navy the outfit of Officer Dibble

Yellow the car to ride to the station,
Purple the face of my father's frustration,
Pink is the shade of a newly born baby,
Black is the night, like an African lady

Grey is the sky on a treacherous day,
Emerald with envy when they get their own way,
Scarlet the blood that is spilled in the battle,
Orange the fur on a highlander's cattle

Golden the honey produced by the bee,
Hazel the eyes that she uses to see,
Silver the hair on a grandfather's head,
Entwined on the fence, is the rose coloured red

LOVE, LIFE, DEATH, AFFECTION, SEDUCTION, DESTRUCTION & EVERYTHING IN BETWEEN

Land of Afar

You're across the ocean, in the land of afar,
You're away from home, but I know where you are,
I wake in the morning, in a cold double bed,
Your place lies empty, with pillow, no head

I sit at the table and stare at your chair,
I look round the room and wish you were there,
I put on my coat; the coat stand is bare,
I stand at the mirror, where you'd brush your hair

I go outside, to the garden you kept,
I go to the park, the place where we met,
I look at your picture; I play your CD's,
I long for you home, but do you long for me?

You're probably courting or being romanced,
If I walked on by, would you give me a glance?
You talk and you text, you call and you write,
But my heart still grows fonder, all through the night

You promised me love, then you took it away,
It feels like forever, you've been gone but a day,
You said you'd stay faithful, in the land of afar,
But all my heart wants is to be where you are

NATHAN SHEPKA

Love or Lust?

What is the difference between love and just lust?
One is a feeling, the other a must,
Walk down the street and clock a fine lady,
Marry a girl and father her baby

Want of the body or want of the soul,
Is it just sex or is marriage the goal?
Keep her eternal, whether poor or of wealth,
Or take her back home for a clean bit of health

Treat her with love; make your world revolve round her,
Or make her earth move when she rips off your trousers,
Caress her sweet face and shower it with kisses,
Or put on a ring and make her your Mrs

Give her your name and declare her your lover,
Or get her too tipsy and sling your leg over,
A bit on the side, love her at your leisure,
Or breakfast in bed after two nights of pleasure

LOVE, LIFE, DEATH, AFFECTION, SEDUCTION, DESTRUCTION & EVERYTHING IN BETWEEN

Take walks in the park and call her "your baby",
Dirty dance in the club til you drive the girl crazy,
Fumble in the dark, a gaze in the park,
Tender young lovers, a meeting of hearts

But is this a fine line that often is blurred?
It is not each man's want, for the best of both worlds?
The love of a woman in his darkest of nights,
And a sweet, loyal wife, who will stay by his side

The first kiss in the rain, to the vigorous bedrock,
To the trip o'er the threshold, when first blessed with wedlock,
From young and wild and in bed half the day,
To pensions and dentures and wrinkles and grey

From the moment their eyes met, from each side of the room,
To the beautiful bride and the dashing young groom,
A candle lit dinner, to the two words, "I do",
From here til forever, I'll always love you

Society's Stain

Raw red grazes an otherwise spotless sky,
Like nosebleed sheets on cancer's bed,
A drop of death drifts in the air,
Like a warning of what lies ahead

Never a day goes by in life,
Without a newspaper fingerprint,
Smudged across Picasso's portrait,
Bad luck blotched in blackest ink

A weed with wicked jagged edge,
Shaped like Antichrist's cruel mouth,
That stains a garden fit for kings,
That's otherwise of sun blessed flowers

The day soon droops with tired eyes,
As corrugated figure hobbles home,
Ignoring spouse's tireless pleas,
To never trek the streets alone

Scuttling sewer rats with Devil's brew,
Fuelled by false rewards of crime,
Liquids mixed by ill-fating hands,
Persuasive poison distilled through time

With toxic breath to wilt a rose,
The stench of rotting liver tastes vile,
The fluttering fear of the choice less passer,
Elderly homeward bound feigns a smile

LOVE, LIFE, DEATH, AFFECTION, SEDUCTION, DESTRUCTION & EVERYTHING IN BETWEEN

Buildings overhead like Reaper's scythe,
As pewter penchant pierces flesh,
Backward blade erupts the spleen,
In sinner's net, the frail enmeshed

Coins clink on callous concrete,
Snatched by evil, fumbling fins,
Scavengers scatter at Skoda suggestion,
Cowardice lies beneath the gin

A simple day of grocery gathering,
About faced to another crime statistic,
Generic headline on page thirty two,
Change the names and then reprint it

Nameless number in darkened ward,
A solitary bed in medical lair,
Grumbling nurse at the sound of a buzz,
Tend to the sores and snow white hair

A view only so far as the rooftop,
No sign of the streets that take life,
Black clouds clam the building,
Where the terminal guest is free of strife

Brutal Blows

Beast in a cage,
Don't let me out,
Your first regret,
I bring the fire,
I bring the hell,
I rent my fists,
So pay the let

Don't rile my fury,
Don't shoot your mouth,
I shoot your head,
A bludgeon bullet,
Pull the trigger,
My fists are guns,
I'm packin' lead

You got a knife,
My wit is sharper,
You don't quite cut it,
I'm a hunter,
Crack the skulls,
Mash the pulp,
Hunt, kill, stuff it

I'm UFC, you're HND,
You've got the cells,
Escape my cell,
I'm in the ring,
Forget the cups,
It's only heads,
On my trophy shelf

LOVE, LIFE, DEATH, AFFECTION, SEDUCTION,
DESTRUCTION & EVERYTHING IN BETWEEN

The red stuff flows,
I see red mist,
Enclosed in mesh,
Break his bones,
My waistline crest,
Fists of fury,
The ref protests

The title won,
You cannot starve,
My fire of flames,
The crowd let out,
Opponent down,
They lie out cold,
Their limbs are lame

A brutal trade,
A trade of blows,
The splattered mat,
Bears both men's blood,
What a way,
To make a living,
I bathe in a blood bath,
Most unforgiving

Inside Out

A calm outer exterior, a face unfazed,
By harsh remarks or wondering gaze,
A weathered soul, jaded much too soon,
Creased with a constant inner frown,
Paintings on the wall, red and blue,
A warm glow streaked with cold,
To rival the most unforgiving winter day,
Deep strokes of distress, a heavy hand,
Led by heavy heart I guess,
Sunken canvas with the score of brush,
A flitting moment of rage on paper,
The anarchy loose upon the page,
A quiet room where only brief light is allowed,
No trespassers to pry, with cunning eyes,
Secrets shed in watercolours,
A painting only the author understands,
Demons released in acrylic exertions,
Broad sweeps of vivid tone, a thrashing storm,
Punish the page, allowed to scatter in the silence,
Under lock and key from the world—I'm me,
Free to talk to the only one, who really listens,
Understanding every letter, no apologies made,
For subjects broached within confines of the mind,
My song only sung in the shower,
Dreams stay in my slumber, undercover,

LOVE, LIFE, DEATH, AFFECTION, SEDUCTION, DESTRUCTION & EVERYTHING IN BETWEEN

Where I'm free to be the man of my will,
A duvet that's bulletproof, deflecting rounds,
Warning off a grizzled bear or murderous blade,
Silly really, but a haven where I'm safe,
Head runs riot with carefree thoughts,
Of stardom, respect and all round applause,
But when I wake, it's different,
Back to reality and back to black,
To blend into the dark, soul unexposed again,
In public a padlock strapped across a diaphragm,
The fears and tears and comments locked away,
Frightened to say, to look the heroes in the face,
A bold, daring outer exterior, a face unfazed,
Confident shell glows like floodlights,
Light up my darkest corner,
But they aren't welcome there, steal the limelight,
Shy wit left in the shadows, my wasted voice,
I could shine like all those others,
If not for fear of break and blunder,
Steal my thunder? No, it's not on show,
It commands a page, on tranquil wall,
For my eyes only, no critical stare,
Release only a pleasant smile, to please,
Enough to see me through a day,
Without the spotlight falling on me,

Subtle, small talk, not rigged to impress,
Or raise anymore than compulsory laugh,
A made-up recording for mundane joke,
A canned laugh, save the real thing,
I'll save my real jokes, I'll laugh later
While on landscape of the evening,
A punching bag for quill and spill,
Ferocity framed like an autobiography,
Dark and distressed, yet a wonder,
In its own right and time,
No clichéd carbon copy like the other sheep,
Afraid of oneself unless on one's own,
One day I'll turn myself inside out,
And let them see the real charade,
They all so deftly practice themselves
Not second nature to me,
Choreographed confidence in majestic manner,
No slip of the tongue in accomplished conversation,
Smile, wink and spring in their step,
All laid out like a proud buffet,
Feast your eyes on the alpha,
But not on the flower unable to bloom,
Wallflower in the room, entrance goes unnoticed,
Alas, another day inside myself,
It's always a case of tomorrows the day

LOVE, LIFE, DEATH, AFFECTION, SEDUCTION,
DESTRUCTION & EVERYTHING IN BETWEEN

Dying Love

Tepid tea and carelessly burnt toast start the morning,
Tender awaking kiss been reduced to heartless yawning,
The words I love you never pass the lovers' lips,
And desire fades with every plateful on the hips,
Whilst extra pounds are gained and firm transforms to folds,
Pounds lost down the sofa, worth its weight in gold,
The bed unmade because both halves decline to bother,
Evening meal is served with loneliness not one another,
Their bodies cloaked in coldest nights with soulless sheet,
Instead of two foot trek to centre bed to meet,
The grass knee high and once great garden overgrown,
A bush once with rose, now blooms consumed with jagged thorns,
Obligatory mid February card with yearly lessening kisses,
Daily compliments and maidenly blush replaced with resentful disses,
Heartfelt words and sexy talk on dirty bits,
Relegated to the trash like overplayed 80's hits,
The words don't mean a thing no more, too often said,
A home is now a house, a place to eat and rest,
The love gone cold like a summer night in paradise,
The number one is at the top, love rolls the dice,
And lovers split like thunder splits a stormy sky,
Their independence makes a winter's day of 4th July,
And brows are furrowed through the years of dying love,
They sing apart, together they don't strike a chord,
As both souls wonder if their pledge was ever true,
When standing in the church repeating words "I do"

෨෭ൟ

Staggered Speech

She occupied the corner booth,
Detective eyes were playing sleuth,
To seek out all like minded hearts,
And then inspect their private parts

Players think they're home and dry,
Soon cast away like swatted flies,
My mortal words before the judge,
Her love I hope she won't begrudge

But can I make my shy approach?
And hope for smile without reproach,
Receiving me with open arms,
Will she dismiss attempted charm?

Beginning lines in strict rehearse,
Present a perfect opening verse,
Scrutinise each syllable,
Recite at cocksure decibel

But why do hands sustain a shiver?
And every note enslave a quiver?
It's not as if I'm going to be,
Getting down upon one knee

Her pretty face soon stalls advance,
As with this girl I have no chance,
No matter what is in my mind,
It won't come out that way inclined

LOVE, LIFE, DEATH, AFFECTION, SEDUCTION, DESTRUCTION & EVERYTHING IN BETWEEN

A murmur, mutter, mispronounced,
Upon which blushing rush will pounce,
My stammers come in shy abundance,
To make my sweet talk sound redundant

But as she rises but to leave,
A stolen sec I wish to thieve,
I ask her over for a drink,
Without a thought of what she'd think

She parks her bottom next to mine,
And orders up two gins and lime,
My words delivered in confidence,
She relishes all my compliments

Her bottom's down, now bottoms up,
I'm drinking from her loving cup,
She listens intent to pleasant words,
Just us two in our separate world

Her long blonde hair is neatly groomed,
She looks at me with baby blues,
She sips her drink with lushest lips,
And strokes my face with fingertips

But as she speaks of her desires,
And toned physique I close admire,
She then looks somewhat mortified,
As in her drink floats her glass eye

Miles Away

A view from the window, of a stretching field,
Sprawls lazily like Sunday morning snooze,
Curved like a model on posing perch,
Rain falls in awakening urgency,
The scent is fresh like the world before,
Unspoilt by all the unnatural fogs,
Of machines burning with toil and tar,
A glucose gulp from a lairy bottle,
As I breathe in the birch and bark,
And each leaf cries its own tear,
Palm facing the sky, not to test the water,
But to feel it fresh against my flesh,
The sky is grieving but it comforts me,
My eyes rest like enveloped in eiderdown,
Yet I feel cool with the outdoor a/c,
Another summer day in Scotland,
But a million miles away I now lie,
The sense of lying on a radiator,
As I sink into the Spanish sand,
Eyes shut to the sun, eyelids glow orange,

LOVE, LIFE, DEATH, AFFECTION, SEDUCTION, DESTRUCTION & EVERYTHING IN BETWEEN

Sand is warm like a smooth silk shirt,
Baked until golden and teen blemishes fade,
The girls lie like goddesses,
Healthy glow and sea blue bikini,
Skin fresh and hair like a fountain,
Flows down the back like waterfall,
Fine figures flirt with the waves,
I look on and smile, sigh but not with stress,
No hustle and stops as patience wears,
Waiting for the red light's extinguish,
Or bug ridden old bastard with uncoordinated effort,
From woolen frayed jumper to go faster trousers,
Perfection in three sixty degree, mistakes are misplaced,
And the swig of quid cider,
At the back of a smog shouldered bus,
A breath of sea air instead of exhaust,
But a week in the year, when all trouble is lost,
In favour of rest under radiant rays,
And the spoil of the city, but miles away

Mr Lover

I'm Mr Lover,
King of kink,
Like no other,
Cheeky wink,
One hot mother,
I'm the daddy,
Under the cover,
Red hot radar,
Aphro's brother,
Spread the funk,
The ladies love it,
Count the notches,
Not the blotches,
Love bite central,
Grab the hotties,
Balling hard,
Loving long,
Don't stop now,
Macho strong,
Love song play,
Sing along,
Tick tock baby,
My sex bomb,
Say's tenor Tom,
First I love 'em,
Then I'm gone,
I'm worth the wait,
Those heaven's gates,
Her parting gift,
Open wide,
Let me in,
I spread my grin,
They spread their legs,
Them girls collate,
They take the bait,

LOVE, LIFE, DEATH, AFFECTION, SEDUCTION, DESTRUCTION & EVERYTHING IN BETWEEN

The juices flow,
Niagara falls,
My engine stalls,
Viagra boost,
King of the roost,
They love the cock,
My parties rock,
Them haters talk,
They last year's stock,
I kiss, they tell,
My body sells,
Like hot potatoes,
It markets well,
Hot off the press,
I give them less,
They ask for more,
Them greedy girls,
Show them the door,
Out of the bed,
Ends on the floor,
They want me nude,
I'm one cool dude,
I brush them off,
I sing Hey Jude,
They like the Beats,
But she's a crawler,
I big dem up,
Now I feel smaller,
Inflate my ego,
Blow it up,
They wanna dance,
I shut the club,
Them clubbers frown,
I take them out,
Their panties wet,
I take them down,
The King of swing,
I got that crown,

I ride the front,
Sit on the throne,
They in the back,
They going home,
I am the taxi,
Pay the fare,
They bite my neck,
They pull my hair,
I'm having seconds,
Then dessert,
And when we done,
A cigarette,
They fall asleep,
I stay alert,
I rare to go,
A one man show,
See me live,
Watch me go,
I race like Schu,
My race car blue,
It's just a blur,
When next to you,
I put it in,
I turn the key,
I turn them on,
They see in me,
A lover sweet,
They got my key,
They want to keep,
They lock me up,
I like it rough,
I like dem chains,
I like dem cuffs,
Now I'm chuffed,
Cos I'm da man,
I'm Uncle Sam,
The Council boss,
I run the land,

LOVE, LIFE, DEATH, AFFECTION, SEDUCTION, DESTRUCTION & EVERYTHING IN BETWEEN

I deal my hand,
I get them tanned,
I get them toned,
They hot as hell,
I make them moan,
They sing my praise,
I watch them gaze,
I'm out of time,
They'll have to wait,
The sun is up,
They came too late,
And in the morn,
Them girlies yawn,
While Mr Lover,
Mows his lawn,
I cut they grass,
They kiss my ass,
The great pretender,
Body lender,
Three day bender,
Their love received,
Cos they the sender,
My beds a blender,
Ménage a trios,
One last hurrah,
Put them to shame,
They round the bend,
They love my love,
They queue in lines,
That way inclined,
I done my time,
Now answer phone,
There's no hello,
My love is out,
I gotta go

Mother's Search

Patterned plates perched on surrounding walls,
Their circumference depicts the changing seasons,
Kettle whistles like the morning paper,
Frail old hand pours her dozenth cup,
According to her, the face of reason and wisdom,
There ain't no problem in life that can't be solved,
With a few tea leaves in a dainty mug,
If only the company came with the cup

Her only problem is an empty fortress,
A bare three seater sofa, a space to fill,
Long-gone lovers and sons and daughters,
Pastures new called like free sweet shop candy,
Whether plains of Africa or city stench,
They came and gone, like the seasons on plates,
A fresh bed, morning meal, for decade or two,
Mother left long behind with remains of the stew

Not a letter nor card or even a footnote,
Birthdays come and go without belated after-thought,
No use to the office for want of a job,
No use to old cronies, desire dried up,
So the days are spent and the sand runs through,
How long to go? If only she knew,
Stiff arm struggles apples from the Bramley tree,
And a lick of paint on the rotting fence

LOVE, LIFE, DEATH, AFFECTION, SEDUCTION, DESTRUCTION & EVERYTHING IN BETWEEN

What holds it all together? Fence and faces,
The last scent of will, reluctance to hoist,
The white flag on the flag pole,
And declare your right to surrender forever,
But the mile to the store with rust ridden cart,
Meets a lonely old stranger playing similar part,
A cane topped with brass falcon and rippled smile,
Join in the labour of the once lonely mile

Each day they trek together, the ravaged track,
Not asking many questions, in case of undesired answers,
But each week like clockwork, the rippled smile,
They drag both feet and baskets to market in town,
But as often as the moon is full, good comes bad,
One week in the spring the stranger was gone,
Make the trip alone and hope for the best,
But with each absent week, hope became less

The seasons rolled by like the patterned plates,
Or the steel spokes on the morning paper,
But the path remained featureless like Africa's plains,
Will the stranger be there when next week comes around?
But fate being fate the old lady passed,
Buried by great nephew and irregular neighbour,
But fate also being fate, God left her in good hands,
Her plot in the ground was beside her frail stranger
Peace is hers with company that is forever

NATHAN SHEPKA

Winter's Wrath

The summer gone with quickening speed,
The summer blooms are choked by weeds,
One thing on which you can depend,
Is all good things come to an end,
A country walk or careless day,
No sooner here than snatched away,
The promise of a young romance,
Is killed with fickle jealous glance,
The winter creeps with iron cool,
Then tames the blow with cosy Yule,
But what of all the years that passed?
Do memories melt or ever last?
The days grow short, the nights go long,
Now hear me sing my autumn song,
The trees go bare and shed their sheets,
My autumn song, for all to hear,
A song so sad the hardy cry,
Weep with eyes that never dry,
For winter's passed with heartless sleet,
But half the cold I choose to keep,
Part of the past I can't let go,
It doesn't melt like winter snow,
A corner where sun never shines,
And burdens be forever mine,
As summer comes around once more,
I keep the key to my heart's door,
Whilst sunshine greets the clearest sky,
My head can't help but question why,
If I'm so good and kind and quaint,
Why am I stained with blackest paint?
A foul streak of winter's wrath,
Paves otherwise a sinless path,
A grudge I hold but deep within,
Smile held together with fragile pin,
As love betrayed me once before,
I'm stuck in winter ever more

LOVE, LIFE, DEATH, AFFECTION, SEDUCTION,
DESTRUCTION & EVERYTHING IN BETWEEN

Waiting for Heaven

Tired of living in decaying streets where concrete gathers mould,
And the souls have all been sold, for a greedy bag of gold,

Tired of my will being met with hearts congealed with cold,
What do sainted skies behold? All their stories still untold,

I'm ready to climb golden stairs and pass through golden gates,
I hope heaven's worth my wait, and my loved ones congregate,

A place where all the guilty free and wounded aren't ill,
Silver song from blackbird's bill, forever on my window sill,

And the music plays in endless loop as lovers dance away,
Angel eyes don't break their gaze, a moonlike gentle haze,

And the murderers and conquerors are absolved of all their sins,
And their twisted ways forgiven, when they shed their poisoned skin,

And the angels play a sacred note upon a golden harp,
To repair all broken hearts, love no longer kept apart,

And anyone goes anywhere without the fear of death,
Lungs are filled with purest breath, and all the babies have been blessed,

Their stolen years are lived upon the magic sun kissed sky,
Parents keep a watchful eye, should the roaming bairns cry,

And the fallen heroes of the war are back with their brigade,
And their sacrifice repaid, for their part in hell's charade,

And the blind and deaf can see and hear, their senses are restored,
Scent and sight of all adored, and the paradise explored,

The old and frail drink from the grail and youth is theirs again,
No more wrinkled, rough terrain or age's elementary pains,

And the bracken grows around the pillars white as purest white,
Daytime never turns to night, pilgrims soak up heaven's light,

And the hungry sit to hearty bread with holy trinity,
Fruits fill the whole vicinity, and love lasts to infinity,

And the close of day brings still a light that shines with comfort glow,
In Satan's yard no flowers grow, in heaven's heart it never snows,

Have a heart and you'll be granted to the kingdom in the sky,
Live in sin and hope to die, live with love and hope to fly,

Here's to a better place, free of all the cruelties of purgatory,
We live merely in God's waiting room, bide your time,
Be free as mine, and true happiness will come,

Amen

Epilogue

The content of this book has been plucked from a variety of sources, mainly the unfrequented corners of Wikipedia where I realised no one would look so it didn't matter if I rampantly pilfered it to save some time. The rest of it, well, that was pulled from the far corners of my mind, which is of astonishingly small dimension.

Those who know me would probably have been quite surprised, not by the utter dross spewing from this book, but by the darkness of the material. To those who don't know me, I will probably have came across as a sour faced, pessimistic shit but if you read the intro and this little paragraph here, cleverly called the epilogue to make me look smarter than the average retard, (I would have called the Introduction the Prologue, but I thought that would have been a step too far,) I come across as a slightly sarcastic, self mocking joker.

The difference in the poems to the man himself is simple—I'm a good actor. De Niro ain't got shit on me; I could have made a better Scarface in my sleep. But I'll let you work out which one is the real me. Just like this book you probably had to work out what some poems were actually going on about. I was going to provide a little "authors explanation" with every piece and then I realised, some things are better left a mystery or to individual interpretation.

Congratulations for finishing my first book and if you skipped to this page just to receive my warm congratulations, go back and read it properly you lazy bastard.

Yooouurs Truuulyy,

Sheppy B-)